JAMES PACK

BLACK CHAOS

Poetry Titles by James Pack

Cats, Coffee, Catharsis
Men are Garbage
Pariah Bound: The Lonesome Poetry

Other Titles by James Pack

The Morbid Museum (Short Stories)
Mushaburui: A Mental Health Journey (Nonfiction)
The Tommy Gun (Novella)

For the friends I hurt when I was drowning in the chaos.
For the friends I lost. I hope we meet again.

Contents

Black Chaos

The Monster Glows in the Night

Orange haze hovers
In the night sky
Rage saunters through the streets
The beginning of the end of things
Or is it the end of
Something starting –
Change is coming
Whether we want it or not
I understand what people thought
During the protests and riots
Of the 1960s
The heavy air strangles US
Fueling the rage monster –
Cutting off oxygen
Doesn't kill this fire
The burning prevails
And the orange haze hovers
In the night sky

Wounded – No Connection

Healing –
I don't know what that is
Stuck in survival mode
Relaxation –
I don't know what that is
War rages inside me
Trapped in my memories
Anger –
I know what that is
Some days it's all I know
Alone –
I know what that is
No support or understanding
A broken soul rises
Pain –
I know what that is

When You've Nowhere to Go Except the Beyond

The ceiling crawls toward the desert
My brain summersaults to a new place
The bed melts away

Pigeons are angry this time of year
But I've never seen them in the desert
The journey is long and hot
I don't know my destination
But somehow I know the way
The sand spirals in a whirlwind

Summersaults again
The kitchen is dull with
Brutal fluorescent lights
I search for a cup but the cabinets
Are all filled with shredded newspaper
I expected this but never think why

Fingers and hands ooze from the sink
I'll need these and the newspaper
For when the pigeons retaliate

A Moment Breathless

The light kisses their pale skin
I long to touch it
A moment frozen in time
Breathless –
They cover their
Imperfections with darkness
I shine more light to see
Caressing in the moment
The warmth I give
Like the Sun to the Moon –
Their body is perfection
Soft and strong
I hold them closer
We share our bodies
Like the Moon shares Sunlight

Friends Leave When You're Awful

Staring at the ceiling
In bed wide eyed, restless
The room sits in darkness
Fortress of solitude –
With no motivation
I overthink my life

With many distractions
I hold no desire
To use or pursue them
Nothing holds interest
If not for work, I would
Never leave my fortress

No films or shows to watch
I'm not interested –
I don't feel the music
Reading feels tedious
The social media
No longer holds value

No meeting new people
No more trying new things
Apathy fills the dark
Lethargy holds the room
Staring at the ceiling
I overthink my life

Cooking in the Desert Heat

I search my pantry
I find beans and rice
And pasta and broth
I don't feel like making anything
Too hot to cook or bake
Within the fridge
Carrots and celery
And eggs and milk
These aren't the snacks I crave
I repeat the ritual
Opening pantry and fridge
As the emptiness grows within
Until I force myself
To endure the heat
Forcing myself to act normal
Forcing the darkness out

A Mermaid Pair

I fear I've ruined something
The greatest thing I ever had
I've lost it and can't get it back
The two people I was closest to
I hurt them with my negativity

I wasn't fully aware what I was
Doing but that's no excuse – I know this –
We would talk everyday
And I took them for granted
Festering in the darkness I made

I focus on more positivity
Each day but they were my support system
I miss them – I liked who I was with them
I'll never reclaim that – I feel lost at sea
Swimming for the shore I left behind

All My Keys Don't Have Locks

Blue black barriers
You can't talk to invisible monsters
Needles hold happy thoughts
Bottles carry the anger
Suitcases weigh two tons
Dreams only come true if you buy them
The kitty cat kicks around the conundrum
Who has time for fairy tale partners
The tattooed trees don't speak anymore
Death's doorknob dangles
The sidewalk's grift is flawless
I want the boardgame to end

And Behold a Black Horse

I made my cry to the universe
Hope in my eyes and fear in my mind
Would anyone hear or answer
Or did it vanish into the ether
It's like writing a letter
And never getting a reply
Is this what the end of days feels like
Is this Famine, the third horseman

Everything collapses around us
Some never learned how to survive
My life is all I have left to lose
Meaning there is nothing left to fear
Light still shines in all this darkness
Hope survives when all is despair
Be kind to others in the end times
Don't fill your last days with hate

Through Hate They Took Power

Every morning I wake
To some atrocity
The news would have us fear
Viruses – Violence –
Tyranny – Fascism –

Many want to believe
Things are getting better
Oppression awaits us –
Every single person

Your white privilege makes
You the last target not –
Free from the oppression
When you realize what the
Whole world is becoming
It'll be too late to stop

There is a coup against
Us by the government
Will you submit or fight –
Will you allow them to
Control and dominate

I Don't Want to be Angry

I don't want it anymore
It's too great a burden
The animosity
The disgust
I feel it too much
People I've hurt
I don't know why they stick around
Or am I the one sticking around
But I can't leave
Not yet, not until
I make amends
If they don't want that
I have to accept their decision
I can't be angry if they
Don't want to hear the apology

Breaking the Shell to Blossom

Looking back on
Past mistakes
Past transgressions
Reflecting on
What was and
What could have been

Memories are eternal
Even if forgotten
They can return
The past doesn't change
The pain was lived
And left a stain

Ignoring the darkest parts
Will cause you to relive them
I try not to sulk
But learn from the darkness
Embracing your cracks
Will let the light in

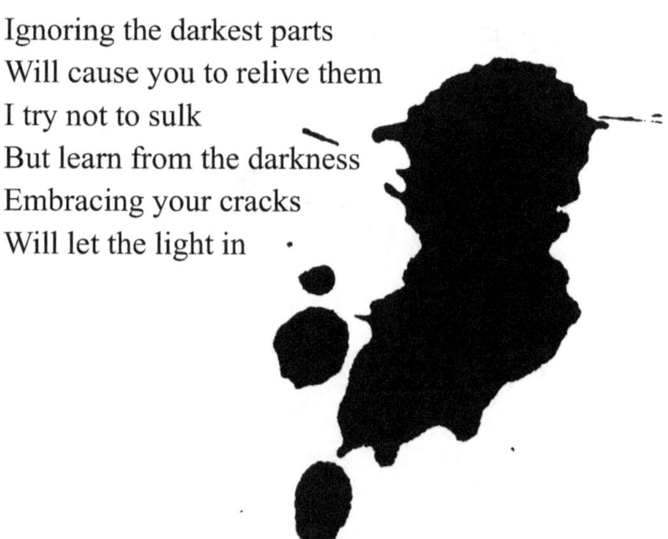

Light My Fire

I stoke my fire alone –
I have no one to
Share this warmth
I feel the comfort
And pleasure of touch
But it is my own
And lacks a certain
Exciting tremble –
To have another
Stoking my inner flames
As I unfold
Flower petals
Is a dream and feeling
I have forgotten –
I stoke my fire alone
To images of others
Embracing –
A sad reminder
Of what I've lost
The burning in another

Black Chaos

The black chaos
Drips on the page
Nightmares live in
Reality –
I release the
Fears through my pen
They never leave
But they have lost
Their hold on me –
A past mended
With ink and words –
With my poems
I capture it
My depression –
A reminder
Of what I was
When black chaos
Consumed my soul

Battle With the Brain Noise

It's a daily battle
Feeling negative or
Feeling irritable
Sometimes I catch myself
Before I lose control
The anger stays with me
For hours or for days –
For positivity
I fight against my thoughts
I struggle to maintain
A mask of happiness
Seeking out distractions
To stop me from thinking
Thoughts can be dangerous –
Brain noise that never ends
My own self-destruction
I am the creator
Of my Heaven or Hell

Self-Isolation

Some fear the storm inside
Been living with mine since October
Some days are still hard
Grief created from my disaster
The pain never goes away
I manage each day a little better
I focus on tasks and distractions
They make the hurt feel lighter
The rain soaks everything inside
Hidden behind my eyes with thunder
I was hurting before the virus came
And I fear hurting another

I Climbed Out the Black Hole Into Sunshine

I have never
Been afraid of
Solitude
I enjoy time to
Myself and the
Solitary activities

I come across
Boredom now and
Then but
That's not what
Hurts the most
When alone

It's that I
Almost never
Hear from anyone
Else
No calls or
Messages

I may speak
To friends or
Family once
Or twice a
Week if
At all

I've tried to
Start conversations
They never last
Long
Invitations
Are a rare thing

In the past
I was bitter
And resented
Everyone
Does anyone
Like me

I faced those
Demons
Loneliness is
Gone so foreign
To not obsess
Over everything

I'm at peace
With myself
I cherish when
I do hear from
Someone
I stay positive

Backstage Concert

The blue hue on the
Black Violin
Light beams shine
In the haze
Noises lured by the
Anticipation
A cacophony
Sound waves thriving
Picking humming
Vibrating thumping
Hidden in darkness
Behind bright lights

Eighty Days

I know you haven't
Counted the days like I have
Is your life any
Different without me there
Was I forgotten

On my long journey
To happiness and healing
I have thought of you
And how I could make amends
To apologize

The one thing I fear
Will you listen if I speak
Or have you moved on
Is it worth the effort to
Wait and hope to reconnect
I may never know

So I wait and hope
Am I a fool for trying
Was I ever worth your time
Was I important
Do you fear speaking to me
The one thing I fear
So I wait and hope

Sometimes Getting up is Courageous

I fear
Being ignored
Forgotten and alone
Do I exist if I'm not seen

I fear
Getting close to
Or comfortable with
Someone because I might hurt them

I fear
I will not heal
And live trapped in the past
Surviving but never living

I fear
Not death but life
Why is living so hard
Every day I face these fears

I fear
Courage will end

Moving on From Hurt and Pain

The past can't be changed
     I don't want to
     But it's all I know –
     I don't know how
     To build a future
     From nothing

The future holds all possibilities
     I can't decide which
     To choose and which
     To avoid –
     Those possibilities
     All come so slowly

The present is boring and tedious
     You want it to end
     But if it does
     The future ends too –
     The present is hard
     To live with a bad past

Having Tea With My Demons

The world inside myself
Is less terrifying
Six months since my fall from grace
My identity shattered
I built myself anew
Phoenix from the ashes
I always fear a relapse
Falling into old habits
I try not to forget
The things that brought me here
I spend more time inside my head
Where I live with my demons not
In fear of what they will do

Flower in a Dead Garden

An attractive flower
Has bloomed in my garden
A mix of pink and white
I water it daily
As it basks in the sun
Thriving in shade and light

All else in my garden
Is barren, dry, and dead
I don't work to revive
The wasteland in my yard
I focus to keep my
Little starburst alive

Despite all my care and
Attention for my love
It has withered away
I feel I've nothing left
I sink into nothing
Crying as my heart sways

I force myself to rise
And begin reviving
Making the whole yard grow
So many trees and grass
A thriving oasis
But the process is slow

As the yard flourishes
My home lays in shambles
Neglected like my yard
I sit in the fine grass
And wonder what when wrong
When did life get so hard

I watch the other homes
On my block down the street
A world engulfed in flames
Nothing I do will help
The flames come my way and
Nothing will be the same

So, I remember my
Beautiful flower
Wishing she was with me
The world lays in shambles
I wonder what went wrong
Wishing she was with me

The Break

The light hum from water falling
An event we always enjoyed
Maybe that's all it ever was
Just a series of moments shared
Trapped in a fading memory
The downpour flooding me with thoughts
We will never dance in the rain
I'll always dream of missed chances
I hope we'll talk again one day

It's a Lonely Place Inside One's Head

I floated inside the empty
Like a dream there was no
Direction or path
One moment morphed into the next
No linear connection
No memories to trace back
Lost in the darkness and no
Desire to escape or leave
Like water I was carried by the ether
No strain on my body but on my mind
Thoughts run amuck in the empty
There's nothing solid to focus or cling to
Only the quiet, beautiful, terrifying
Blackness of nothing
The deep which lives within
Our hearts and souls and minds
A never-ending void
That always finds its way
Back into me

Today is a Gift

Stresses come and go
Feelings come and go
Friends come and go
The only constant
Is you
You are always here
You are always in
The present moment
But you live in the past
And the future
End the anxiety and depression
Live in the present moment
Now is the only
Time that matters

The Light in My Darkness

I've been afraid to sleep
Darkness thrives in nightmares
I've feared being alone
Solitude brings darkness
I've been afraid to get close
Friends pushed away by darkness
I sat with my back to the wall
So, darkness couldn't surprise me

I fear the worst
From my darkness
But the darkest corners
Are in the outside world
Cruelty and hate from others
The darkness of humans overwhelms
My darkness and I
Have come together to survive

Land of the Free; Free to Die

We lose work in a crisis
The pandemic kills business
What do we do when we can't
Afford food or pay our rent
Will the rich finally care
                    No
I don't think they ever will

The Devil Watches as Humans Destroy Themselves

So many years feeling alone
I think I finally understand it
Loneliness has nothing to do with
Not being around others
It's about boredom
Distraction
Companionship makes the passing
Of time so much easier
It feels smaller, less painful
And the best part is
It keeps you out
Of your
Head

                                Demons

There's no time to overthink,
Feel anxious, or depressed
When someone is
Talking to you or
Listening
Books, movies, and hobbies
Only take us so far
The rest of the
Journey is with
Companions

                                Trust issues

It's so easy for many to
Connect and find friendships

To have game nights
And date nights
And parties
Compatriots
Anything to help forget, to help
Ignore that existence is pain
The human superpower
A blessing and curse
To forget
                    Bottled up
I don't want to be among them
These distracted, broken creatures
I want to remember but
Not controlled by the
Memories

I'm not lonely, I'm bored
In need of
Distractions

A Game No One Wins

A child born and
Bred in darkness
Seeking the light but
Only plunging
Deeper into the black
Searching for purpose
And meaning
And answers
Reasons for
Perpetual pain
What is destiny and fate
Social constructs and fantasies
Walking the path
And knowing the path
Are never the same
Answers don't come
Until the end
Existence is pain
The wheel of fate
Crushes us all

A Letter From the Author

I took the advice from some reviewers and went with a shorter collection of poetry. I focused more on the theme to give the collection more substance. Black Chaos is what I call my depression. Each poem in this collection was written after I hit rock bottom and had to seek help to overcome my issues.

It has been over a year since that all happened and I'm still healing. I imagine it will be a lifetime of healing. I've lost some friends along the way. And I've spent more quality time with myself. The poems in this collection were my way of working through some of my issues. It was one step in many to work towards recovery.

If you enjoyed these poems, or if you didn't enjoy them, please write a review expressing how you fell about my work. Feedback is the best thing a writer can receive whether it's good, bad, or indifferent. If you relate to some of these poems, I hope you're working towards recovery. If you can't relate, I hope you never do. Thank you for reading my poetry.

James Pack

About the Author

James Pack has written several collections of poetry and short fiction, is a contributing writer for themighty. com and the Bipolar Writer Mental Health Blog. He studied Theatre Arts at the University of Arizona and studied Entertainment Business at Full Sail University for his graduate degree. James is a board member and Treasurer for the Tucson Fringe Theatre Festival and works with many nonprofits and local artists in the performing arts community. He lives in Tucson, AZ. Visit his website to learn more about James. Thejamespack.com, @jamespackwriter.

James Pack wrote this bio in the third person and it makes him feel narcissistic and gross.

www.ingramcontent.com/pod-product-compliance
Lightning Source LLC
Chambersburg PA
CBHW061727130726
47996CB00006B/2539

9798700276313